SMALL & BEAUTIFUL FLOWER ARRANGEMENTS

SMALL & BEAUTIFUL
F·L·O·W·E·R
ARRANGEMENTS

MARION W. JOHNSON
WITH PHOTOGRAPHS BY
GEORGE CHINSEE

Clarkson N. Potter, Inc./Publishers • NEW YORK
DISTRIBUTED BY CROWN PUBLISHERS, INC.

TO
R. ALAN JOHNSON
JOHN M. BARRETT
DARRELL RIKERT
KNOWL JOHNSON

Title page: One polyantha rose ("The Fairy"), autumn clematis, and blades of blue fescue are in a Santa Clara pot from New Mexico.

Published by Clarkson N. Potter Inc.,
One Park Avenue, New York, New York 10016
and
simultaneously in Canada by General Publishing Company Limited

Printed in Hong Kong by South China Printing Co.

Library of Congress Cataloging in Publication Data

Johnson, Marion W.
Small & beautiful flower arrangements.

Bibliography: p.
Includes index.
1. Miniature flower arrangement.   I. Title.
SB449.5.M56J64   1983   745.92   82-18615
ISBN 0-517-54788-0

10 9 8 7 6 5 4 3 2
First Edition

CONTENTS

*B*everley Nichols, an English writer and gardener, captured the pleasure of miniature flower arrangements in his book *Laughter on the Stairs.* He described the preparation ritual that took place every time Miss Mint was an expected guest:

> There were always special things to be done. . . . [T]here had to be a number of Lilliputian bunches of mixed flowers, placed in strategic positions, on tables and mantelpieces. They were arranged in such containers as silver saltcellars, liqueur glasses, eggcups, and even matchboxes, lined with tin and painted white. Whether Miss Mint enjoyed looking at them as much as I enjoyed making them will always be a moot question. They were certainly among the major pleasures of my life.

Thistle, grass, purple loosestrife, and common persicaria,
all found by an urban highway, are in a pottery vase.

Besides hinting at the variety of containers that lend themselves to cradling charming handfuls of blossoms and greenery, Nichols also revealed the secret of the arrangements in this book: you must do them first and foremost to please yourself.

These are diminutive assortments of easily arranged tiny flowers and leaves. They can be subtle, understated, dramatic, or whimsical. A blossom or two or a sprig will re-create or refresh.

Miniatures are small-scale replicas of larger arrangements with flowers, leaves, and containers proportionately reduced. Save an occasional branch or leaf reaching out an inch or two beyond, most fit comfortably within a six-inch square.

My own enthusiasm for these decorative flights of fancy grew out of a period of time I spent in starchy New England. There, the prevailing adage was "use it up, wear it out, make it do"—and I did, at least when it came to flowers. Thanks to the roadside, the florist, my garden, and occasionally my neighbors, there were always plenty of urns, baskets, and even vases brimming with armfuls of fresh flowers. Still, when the grander arrangements were done and in place, I had side shoots, a modest bud or two, fragments of blossoms, just-unfurled tiny leaves as leftovers. Perhaps influenced by Yankee thrift, I began to pop them into little containers and place them on my writing desk or telephone table. They exuded a charm all their own.

When you focus your attention on small forms, you discover the virtues of what Beverley Nichols described as "shrinking." "To extract the keenest pleasure from [small forms] you must be able to diminish yourself—you must acquire the talent of shrivelling yourself up into a tiny creature that is able to walk, in spirit, under the tiny saxifrages, and shiver with alarm at their heavy weight of blossom, to climb, in your mind's eye, the mossy stones, and grow dizzy on their steep escarpments." He pointed out that some days it is easy to be in a "shrinking" mood and other days "it is terribly difficult to shrink properly. Try as one will, one remains six foot high—a cumbersome human in an overcoat, with cold feet and a trowel." When gathering materials, do try to set aside self-consciousness and think of your goal as a personal, private delight. Remember: these bouquets are filled with exuberance, designed for pleasure. If your first attempt is not pleasing, toss it out, and try another.

The current trend in natural, open, informal arrangements has attracted admirers and attention after what seems like decades of stilted, formula bouquets. Arrangements are freer and anything but staid—an attractive accompaniment to the way most of us now choose to live. Arrangements are enlivened, too, by a taste for the romantic and by Oriental influences. Flowers once ignored as weeds are now appreciated for their gracefulness and have joined more exotic blossoms in current bouquets. Our arrangements have a fresh look, a country garden feeling. We are at home with Oriental asymmetry and have grown to love loose,

Spring flowers—lilac, quince, Scotch broom, tiny carnations, azalea, and miniature daffodils—are displayed in a 3-inch-tall urn.

These golden miniature daffodils
are in a crystal cigarette container.

almost disarranged arrangements. We now appreciate fewer flowers more attractively displayed.

Miniature flower arrangements need the smallest amounts of fresh plant materials. They are also among the least expensive ways of bringing flowers into your house.

The arrangements in this book are but a sampling of what is possible. See them as a gentle nudge, a promise of pleasure to come. They can be used for inspiration or freely copied. Learn from Nature—the original arranger—and study flower and still-life paintings and drawings. They will suggest color combinations, shapes, styles of arrangements, containers, and settings to place them in. One can begin with any one of these elements and build the arrangement from there. Fresh materials are available at little or no effort or expense. Select the ones you love, those that match the mood and qualities you seek. Beautiful, suitable containers are either already at hand or are easily acquired.

All that's needed is a spirit of playfulness, wit, and imagination. The small, diffident flowers, when arranged as miniature bouquets, gain quiet stature and impressive beauty.

A miniature gladiolus can be grown
in the garden or bought at the florist.

Nature is a far better gardener than anyone could dream of being. Gathering what she so freely offers is the easiest and most satisfying way of getting materials for miniature flower arrangements.

To share in the bounty, start near home or any place where things are growing. A stroll along a country road, through fields, woods, or wet areas will yield baskets of material.

Look with your eyes, but do not ignore the other senses. You first might smell flowers that you do not see. Let the scent guide you to their source. Lift low branches or big leaves. The small shoots that work well in small arrangements may be hiding underneath. And watch where you step—some of your best discoveries may be directly under foot. Most small flowers grow on tiny plants close to the ground.

*Honeysuckle with buds and berries was found near a city
early in the fall. The arrangement is in a black china container.*

If there are big trees shading the ground, look for climbing vines. The flowers will be found high up, where they have grown to get sun.

For size, keep in mind that this is all a nickel and dime operation. Flowers that correspond to those coin sizes are about the dimensions you want. Many larger flowers, such as roses and carnations, are available in miniature. Some big flowers made up of tiny florets can also be used.

It helps to wear sturdy footwear and to have your arms and legs covered, because finding flowers often involves getting down on your hands and knees. More often than not, the flower you want most is growing on the other side of a mud puddle, in a thorny patch, down a gully, or up a steep bank. It's hard to say whether it is the flower's attempt at self-protection, a case of the grass being greener elsewhere, or our love of what is just out of reach. Whatever, if you're dressed for it, you needn't be daunted.

In the country in summer one does not have to venture very far to find a choice of flowers and greens that are lively and fresh.

The problem with found flowers is not finding them, but, rather, deciding which ones to take home. What you gather on any given day depends both on what happens to be flourishing and on what strikes you as appealing. Indulge your whims. With the selection of the first few flowers, the bouquet will dictate what else you might want to pick. Build on what you have, perhaps assembling several arrangements at once.

Among my favorite found flowers are two white ones: clematis and columbine. They bloom in summer when white is refreshing and cool to sun-tired eyes. Each is lively, in its own way. The clematis is an energetic burst of gossamer petals. The columbine is subtle and aloof. It is a graceful flower that looks much like a dancer "on pointe," head thrown back. Another of my favorites is the miniature scouring rush. It is not a flower at all, but rather a slim, green spike—a reed—that grows where there is plenty of moisture, near ponds and lakes, even in drainage ditches. It endears itself to the arranger because of its good vertical line.

The city dweller can find flowers as well. The most robust stand of Queen Anne's lace I ever saw was by a highway exit ramp in Brooklyn. It is something special to get free flowers from concrete. Empty lots, cracks in the sidewalk, and the edges of roads and highways are fair game. However, parks, public plantings, and doorway tubs are off limits.

Wild flowers that can be found in cities are Queen Anne's lace, thistle, goldenrod, honeysuckle, purple loosestrife, common persicaria, and common toadflax. Flowers most often thought of as weeds should also not be bypassed, whether growing in an urban or rural patch. However, handle them with much care since they are often more fragile than hothouse or cultivated flowers.

Knowing what one is looking for, and at, often makes finding flowers easier. A good guidebook such as *A Field Guide to Wildflowers* by Roger Tory Peterson and Margaret McKenny, is helpful. (See the Recommended Reading List for further suggestions.)

Goldenrod and common toadflax, wild flowers found in the city,
are arranged in a terra-cotta container that rests on a slab of stone.

*A ¼-cup copper measure holds
cornflowers and their foliage.*

More enjoyable than a guidebook is a person familiar with local wild flowers. That person, for me, is Evelyn. She lives near a small lake, and not much that grows nearby escapes her. A visit will include a walk along the water's edge so I can see what's blooming there. It might be horsetails, blue vervain, or wild asparagus. One is apt to return to the spot where old favorite flowers were found in previous years, but one quickly discovers Nature's unpredictability. They will not necessarily grow in the same spot year after year. While Evelyn keeps up a steady flow of information, we'll explore the hill behind the house, scrambling under bushes and over walls. She is guided by an educated instinct. Watching her, one becomes aware of just how much time, attention, and devotion are invested in becoming a companion to Nature.

Early morning or late in the day is best for cutting flowers because these are the times when they will contain the most moisture. A bucket or basket outfitted with small water-filled cans helps keep a variety of flowers separate and prevents them from becoming a tangled ruin. A sharp knife or a pair of snips or small scissors is the other essential tool to take along.

Before you cut, learn what flowers are on the conservation lists. These lists change from year to year and vary from state to state. You may not cut these flowers. However, if you find fields of a particular flower, you are probably safe, even if you haven't checked the lists. If there is doubt in your mind, move on.

Careful cutting actually helps many plants produce more blooms. Don't pull or yank at a plant. Cut sparingly from any one plant. Cut at an angle and give yourself a stem that is longer than you think you'll need. In most cases six inches will suffice.

At home, condition your finds to improve their longevity. When a flower is cut from the plant it grew on, you have removed it from its life support system. It needs time and a little help to recover before being placed in an arrangement. Recut the stems at an angle under water and strip off the lower leaves. This exposes a larger number of water-absorbing cells to the water and improves the flower's chances of survival.

Flowers whose stems secrete a milky substance (dandelions, for example) should have their stems sealed by dipping the ends briefly in boiling water or by burning the ends with a match until a callus forms. Asters, irises, and clematis, though they don't have milky stems, will last longer if dipped in boiling water. The flower can be protected from the heat with a wet paper turban.

And last, give the poor things a good drink. The water should not be cold but tepid. Let them stand in plenty of fresh water in a cool, dark, draft-free place for several hours or overnight.

Gardeners are optimists. They act on the chance that next year the roses will smell sweeter, everything will come up on schedule, the plants with which they had nothing but failure will be a success, and there will be enough rain. A gardener thrives on hope—on having better luck next year.

Growing things to some people is easy and to others terribly difficult. We all know people who can kill the hardiest houseplant. What is most necessary to grow anything is to want to do so with head, heart, and soul. Those who find, for whatever reason, that they can't develop even a rudimentary green thumb need not despair. They need only work on their diplomatic skills, which will enable them to secure cutting rights to other people's gardens.

Flowering trees and shrubs produce the right ingredients for min-

An arch of willow over a pansy and a hosta leaf are in a glass candle holder. The wood-block stand is covered with sheet moss.

iature arrangements. In addition to flowers, they have twiggy branches, lively foliage, fall berries. In spring, branches can be forced into early bloom by being brought into a warm room. Vines and ground covers all produce flowers and/or greenery that are useful for arranging. Do not overlook a plant as ordinary as privet. Often used as hedging material, the fragrance of its pure white tiny flower is sublime and its form is delicate and appealing. Use it in miniature arrangements as a prince, not a pauper. The list that follows is a smattering of plants that produce flowers and greenery of the proper scale for miniature arrangements.

TREES: ash; Carolina silverbell; fringe tree; hawthorn; ornamental flowering and fruit-bearing fruit trees (such as apple, cherry, peach, plum); redbud; yellowwood.

SHRUBS: azalea; crape myrtle; deutzia; flowering quince; fothergilla; forsythia; heaths and heathers; kolkwitzia; lilac; mahonia; mock orange; mountain laurel; polyantha roses; roses; spirea; viburnum.

VINES: clematis (*macropetala* and *paniculata*); fire thorn; honeysuckle; winter jasmine.

GROUND COVERS: ajuga; arabis; epimedium; lamium; lily of the valley; mazus; pachysandra; vetch; vinca.

When choosing plants to cultivate, a good nursery catalog will offer more material than most of us will ever have energy or room for. Still, catalogs are excellent source books which provide endless inspiration and temptation to flower arrangers and growers. A selection of catalogs is included in the Recommended Reading List at the end of this book.

Novices will find it easy to go to a local nursery or garden center in spring to buy a few boxes of annuals. Plant them according to directions given on the label or advice offered by the sales clerk. They are a guarantee that you will have something growing. The more adventurous will buy a few packets of seeds, follow planting and cultivating instructions, and wish themselves good luck.

The early spring bulbs are easy flowers to grow. They can be ordered in early summer and planted in the fall.

BULBS: erythronium; glory-of-the-snow; hardy cyclamen; miniature daffodil; snowdrop; striped squill; summer snowflake.

Perennials, like old friends, provide continuity. With some care and attention they will come back year after year. Annuals, like new acquaintances, can be varied from year to year with little investment.

PERENNIALS: alyssum; candytuft; coralbells (even a chartreuse-colored variety); cranesbill (the true geranium); dianthus (pinks); epimedium; forget-me-not; pearlwort; phlox; primrose; St.-John's-wort; sweet woodruff.

ANNUALS: abronia (pink sand verbena); ageratum; alonsoa (mask flower); alyssum; anagallis (pimpernel); anchusa (forget-me-not); asperula (annual woodruff); baby's breath; browallia; chrysanthemum (especially feverfew); creeping zinnia *(Sanvitalia procumbens);* dianthus (which includes pinks and sweet William); diascia (twinspur); gomphrena (globe ama-

One miniature gladiola flower and sprigs of holly flowers and broom are arranged in a pottery vase.

Sprigs of Japanese quince, an enthusiastic bloomer,
cut in February in Virginia and set in an old Chinese container.

ranth); lantana; linaria; lobelia; salvia; schizanthus (poor man's orchid); snapdragon; viola tricolor (pansy).

Both the vegetable patch and herb garden provide hunting grounds for miniature arrangements. Purple basil, for example, will look like beech leaves in a small-scale arrangement. Herbs can be dried and used long after the arrangement is no more.

VEGETABLES: Beans and peas have wonderful flowers if you can spare them (especially early dwarf gray peas with a deep purple velvet flower). Beets; carrots (for their tops); lettuce for tender green leaves; and spinach.

HERBS: Chive; lavender; marjoram; purple basil; tansy; thyme (silver-edged and golden-edged).

A gardener might also try the miniature plants: gladiola; miniature roses; zinnias. No unusual care is required. The size is suited to Lilliputian arrangements. One can also multiply the possibilities for small arrangements by adding the low-growing alpine plants seen in rock gardens.

Those who have no greenhouse, no garden, not even a tiny plot of land can make good use of the sunniest available windowsill. Five varieties of jasmine, each in its own pot; a collection of baby geraniums, or a planter of tiny ferns will do nicely to supplement what you find at the florist.

The white chrysanthemum "Pearl" and a few sprigs of the shrub snowberry (Symphoricarpos) *are in a wooden bucket.*

FLOWERS TO BUY

In the Andes I once saw a mountainside covered in white orchids. I was convinced—at that altitude—that I had gone to heaven. Now, when I go to the florist's and buy orchids, it is still a bit of a miracle.

Good florists deal in very fragile and perishable goods. Flowers are picked or "harvested" one day in North America, Europe, Africa, or South America, and arrive at big-city wholesale flower markets the next.

An arranger's florist is interested and knowledgeable, and imbued with an agreeable disposition. Those who enjoy what they do appreciate informed and loyal customers. If you are faithful and regular, even with small orders, you will get good service. Appreciate the value of your florist's time and ask thoughtful, intelligent questions. Ask for flowers you want but don't see in the shop.

*Freesia and ranunculus were popped
into a silver nut basket.*

Of the small-scale flowers to buy, I particularly like lily of the valley because of its scent, and I consider one stem of flowers and a leaf or two about the best arrangement ever devised. While full-sized gladiola have always looked a bit loony to me, miniature ones are very handsome, with a nice bend at the tip which gives movement to the arrangement.

Other flowers for sale include baby's breath; button chrysanthemums; candytuft; flowering branches; forget-me-not; heather; ixia; statice; tiny carnations. And, of course, remember orchids.

In the dead of winter you can find materials at your greengrocer's or in the produce section in the supermarket. Look for broccoli rabe and celery (leaves); enoki mushrooms; Oriental vegetables; pineapple (leaves); spinach.

Flowers you buy have usually been conditioned. A good florist will tell you whether they need any additional treatment. If they do, recut the stems under water, then let them stand in fresh water before arranging.

There are always new products and schemes that promise to extend the life of cut flowers. If something works for you, use it. Starting with fresh, well-conditioned plant material, clean equipment, and containers is a must. Keeping the arrangement out of drafts and direct light helps, and changing the water daily, or at least replenishing what the flowers drink, will prolong the life of the bouquet. A few grains of charcoal from a plant shop added to the water is helpful in keeping the water sweet.

Enoki-dake, or straw mushrooms, were bought at the Oriental grocery and arranged with bits of moss in a stoneware sake cup. This arrangement improved when the mushrooms began to flop.

*An arrangement of white statice and red miniature carnations in a
black square container, resting on an X-shaped stand and a piece of black Plexiglas.*

White dendrobium orchids, eucalyptus leaves, and a spray of oncidium orchids are combined in a silver container. The stand is a crystal paperweight.

C O N T A I N E R S

Small containers should be chosen with the same taste and care as when selecting larger ones. Beware of the sweet, the cute, and the vulgar. Bad taste is just as poisonous in miniature as it is in full-blown form. Pleasing small-scale arranements command containers that are as strong in shape, design, color, and materials as are vessels worthy of larger arrangements. A good container must hold enough water to feed thirsty flowers. The size of containers for miniature arrangements generally does not exceed a few inches in any direction.

When shopping for them, count on secondhand stores, whether they call themselves antique, resale, or thrift shops. These often blowsy emporia are virtually inexhaustible sources for inexpensive, good-looking containers that can be given away without a second thought. Look for dining table appointments: saltcellars, nut dishes, sweetmeat baskets, urns

*A Santa Clara black-on-black pot from New Mexico, respected as an
art form, is the container for silver thyme and sweet jasmine. The stand is slate.*

A porcelain cherub holds a porcelain basket, which is filled with a small white lace flower, a pink azalea, miniature daffodils, tiny carnations, and fresh dill.

A blanc de chine *figure* becomes a container when wax flowers and
a Peruvian lily are inserted in the hole in her robe where the hand should be.

for short cigarettes, toothpick holders, and schnapps glasses in everything from gold-washed silver to chipped glass.

Stores that specialize in Oriental goods—antiques or souvenirs—have sake cups, water pots, small teacups, sauce and dipping dishes, toothpick holders, water droppers, incense burners, small baskets, and miniature vases.

Museum shops and the United Nations gift shop in New York City are excellent sources for containers, many handmade, from here and abroad.

Housewares departments and cooking equipment shops sell little pans, measures, and tin molds that can also serve as basket liners.

There are craft fairs at every level of taste and artistry. If you don't find the perfect pot, you may very well find someone who will make one to your specifications.

A seashell that holds water and doesn't wobble is a superb one-of-a-kind container. So is a geode or rock with a large enough hole for water (most will need a special stand). Lava stone sold for bonsai will work if it includes a deep depression for water. An interesting chunk of wood is easily made into a container—just bore a hole for water and coat it with wax or give it a nonporous liner.

Porcelain figurines that have a basket or jug look livelier with fresh flowers in these receptacles. Or the figure itself can become the container. Some Chinese *blanc de chine* figures are made with one fragile hand cast separately and later slipped into the hole left in the robe. Some of these figures suffer a lost or broken hand, including the one I own. I cork up the hole on the bottom, fill it with water, and put flowers where the hand should be. It is a bit of trouble—the cork has to be made level on the bottom and the flower stems made to curl down into the water. And after a few flower changes, the cork has to be removed carefully with a corkscrew and the whole process repeated. But I'm very fond of the old dear and find the results well worth the effort.

Throwaway containers—the tops and caps of toiletry bottles, the plastic or metal screw-on or push-on lids and covers of household products—can be used to hold flowers, especially when you want to give away more bouquets than you have vases you'll part with. Improvements can be made by applying paint or by gluing on cord, straw, or other attractive materials.

For centuries the great workers in precious metals, porcelain, and crystal have created magnificent small bowls, cups, and vases. If a piece is very rare, of museum quality and a work of art, it doesn't need flowers. Vases that are a step or two removed from museum pieces are the arranger's true jewels. How one treats these treasures is an individual decision but a liner to protect the inside certainly is recommended.

A R R A N G I N G

A handsome flower arrangement can be assembled intuitively, using good visual sense and a practiced eye. Arranging is nothing more than creating a composition with the basic principles of design. You can demonstrate this by holding the stems of three little flowers—or three sprigs of parsley—loosely in one hand. Move them with your free hand, making the smallest flower the tallest, and the largest the shortest, just above your thumb. Turn one flower to face you, another in profile or three-quarter view. Gently shift the flowers in your hand until they form a pleasing combination, and each is seen to best advantage. It will be livelier if the spaces between the flowers are uneven: two close together and one farther apart from the others. When the three pieces look just right, they will seem to come together as a whole. No one piece dominates or outweighs the others; the eye goes to

Van Gogh's painting of 14 sunflowers was the inspiration for this arrangement of 3 buds and 11 flowers of creeping zinnia (Sanvitalia procumbens).

a focal point and you know this is a pleasing design, a composition of merit.

The plant material will all but tell you what to do with it. It will make the inherent quality of the flowers apparent. If the flowers are straight and stiff, plan to make that a strength. If they bend, wave, and dip, let them tumble over the edge of the container. Accept the flowers as they are without manipulating or forcing them to behave in ways that would never occur naturally. Remember who this arrangement is for and where it is to be placed. The design should be a natural development.

Fill a container half full of fresh cool water and decide which stem will be the tallest one in the arrangement. This one goes in first. A general rule of thumb is that the container is about one-third of the completed arrangement's height. Judge the correct height by holding the flower next to the container. Cut off the excess at an angle and place the stem toward the center of the container if the arrangement will be seen from all sides or from above. If it will be seen from the front and sides, the stem should be placed near the back edge of the container.

From this single stem you will find it easy to determine proportions for the rest of the arrangement. The next flowers should determine the width and additional flowers or foliage will fill out where necessary.

If a flower has too many leaves, remove some. This is "grooming." You may not like the leaves at all—in that case remove them entirely and substitute something else. A few blades of grass do very nicely.

If you are unsure about what to add or subtract to get the effect you want, use the principles of design for guidance.

• In any design the eye looks for a resting place, a focus. It may be one flower or several together toward the center of the arrangement and usually slightly above the rim of the container. An arrangement without focus looks busy and will not hold attention.

• For a sense of unity, the plant materials must make sense together. In practice this means avoiding flowers of widely varying sizes, shapes, textures, seasons, and types. Lilies of the valley and sunflowers, for instance, will never work together.

• An arrangement should not look top-heavy or as though it is about to fall over from too much weight on one side. It should appear balanced. Without actually weighing objects, our eyes tell us that there are differences in weight.

• Flowers also have visual weight. The larger they are the heavier they appear, and dark colored flowers are weightier than light colored ones. One or two dark flowers will balance a batch of little pale ones. The tallest should be smaller and lighter than those toward the bottom to avoid a top-heavy look. The farther an element is from the imaginary center, the greater its visual weight. This is most important with asymmetrical arrangements. A single far-reaching stem must be counterbalanced by several centered dark ones or many central light ones.

• Colors have personalities and characteristics of their own. Yel-

The wood rack of a soap dish is the holder for three dendrobium orchids. A slate ink stone from Japan holds the water.

A shaped piece of foam, fitted in a brown bonsai saucer, is secured with two strips of cloth florist's tape, and covered with sheet moss. A tiny maidenhair fern almost hides three primroses.

low is very strong when combined with other colors and can easily outshine them. To keep it from being an overwhelmer as well as to give it freedom, I like to use yellow by itself, with other yellows, or mixed with whites that act as reflectors. If I do want to mix other colors with yellow, flowers whose colors are deeper and darker than yellow work best. Blue does the opposite of yellow: it gets shy and retiring in a mixed arrangement. What blue needs is light—light to be seen in and no dim corners.

The colors of flowers can clash and compete with each other, and the more colors you work with in an arrangement, the greater the chance of a color riot. There are times when one wants that feisty spirit, but to keep it under control the simplest trick is to use gray-green foliage around and among the flowers.

The art of arranging is knowing when to stop. Generally it is best to err on the side of too little rather than getting hopelessly entangled in an overdone arrangement. When the arrangement is finished, consider it in its setting and add no more flowers, although a stand or accessory may enhance the arrangement and its surroundings.

A few tools and holders will prove to be necessities. Once the plant material is conditioned and ready to be arranged you should have a selection of the following equipment within reach.

A good, sharp knife or pair of snips is the arranger's most vital tool. It should be chosen for its comfortable weight and balance in the arranger's hand. What is *not* wanted is anything that will crush the stem as the cut is made (like a dull pair of scissors) since this injures the water-absorbing cells in the stem and severely limits the arrangement's longevity. I have used a pair of bonsai shears for years and find them superb and comfortable. Many arrangers use a florist's knife, which is similar to a jackknife with a rounded point. A well-supplied garden center will have a variety of choices.

A small hammer is useful for bashing woody stems, thereby increasing their water-absorbing potential. Any hammer that can be handled comfortably will serve well.

A pair of tweezers whose ends have been dipped in melted wax (to create a soft, edge-free surface) helps in handling very small fragile flowers. Chopsticks work well for this purpose, too.

An eyedropper is a precise, nondisruptive tool for adding and removing water from miniature containers. Long, slim ones are available at chemical supply houses and are often easier to use than short, stubby ones.

A fine sprayer, whether specifically intended to mist flowers or just a clean, general purpose spray bottle, provides a gentle mist to keep the flowers fresher longer.

*Three fiddlehead ferns and bits of moss in a white china
snail sit on black pebbles and a black glass stand.*

An arrangement for a bathroom shelf contains vinca leaves, grape hyacinths, and pachysandra flowers and leaves. The container is an irregularly shaped saltcellar.

Materials to hold fresh flower stems in place in their containers are basically the same as those one would use for larger arrangements. One only needs to find smaller versions or use less of any given material.

Water-absorbent foam can be cut and sculpted to fit virtually any container (Oasis and Quickie are two well-known brands). Once a piece has been cut, it is important to soak it thoroughly in water first, then fit it into the container. Most stems will pierce the material and slide into place easily.

A *skewer or toothpick* from the kitchen helps poke holes in foam when stems cannot pierce it.

Pin holders, also called needlepoint holders, may be bought in gardening supply stores and come as small as seven-eighths of an inch in diameter. They are placed in the container and flowers are impaled on the pins. (The weight of these holders helps stabilize the container in addition to holding the flowers.) This method is especially good when not many stems are being used, but each stem has to be thick enough to be stuck onto a pin.

Floral clay is employed to hold the pin holders firmly in place. It is waterproof and will stick to most surfaces (apply and stick before water is added). It will not stain silver or leave a mark.

Plastic netting—the type supermarkets use to cradle grapes—can be used in several ways. Wadded up, it helps hold thin, delicate stems in an opaque vase. Rolled and then curved into a doughnut shape, the netting can provide support around the inside perimeter of the container for flowers placed in the doughnut hole. You can wrap netting around an arrangement created in your hand, and the entire ensemble—netting and all—can then be put into the container. Wadded-up netting can also be used much like foam to provide support when stems are stuck through its holes.

Brass, copper, or green-coated florist's wire can be crumpled and stuck to the bottom of the container with florist's clay. It provides the arranger with a made-to-fit wire structure to stick the flowers into. Fine brass chicken wire commonly used as grillwork for furniture doors could be used in the same way. Check cabinet hardware makers to find some.

Pebbles can be used to hold stems or to cover up the holder that does hold them. The tiny ones used in aquariums are suitably sized, but good sense dictates leaving the madly colored ones for the fish.

A thin strip of lead is also useful. One end can be bent around the stems of flowers while the other end is hooked on the lip of the container. This works well if one wants the stems gathered to one side of the container.

S E T T I N G S

*M*iniature flower arrangements are not soloists but are meant to be part of a setting, an ensemble of background, surface, accessories, and surrounding objects. The arrangement in its setting should look not artificial but natural, not contrived but whole. This is for the designer to orchestrate.

Small flowers gain stature when placed with objects of small scale or where there is a step up of sizes. They are best seen at close, intimate range. They belong in settings where the distance from arrangement to viewer closes out much of the visual world beyond it. The viewer and arrangement should share a private world for a moment or two.

There is no lack of settings that permit personal viewing. Flowers accompanying food and drink come to mind first. Small-scale arrangements add special delight to daily family meals or dinners enjoyed alone.

*Flowering quince is in a glazed
pottery container on a library shelf.*

The sink top or toothglass holder in bathrooms is ready-made for small flowers (and flowers thrive on the abundance of moisture that jeopardizes most other accessories). Writing tables, desks, telephone stands are also obvious choices, as are dressing tables. These are often crowded working sites which may require placing the arrangement at eye level on a small wall bracket above the fray. Small niches found in some stairwells are self-contained worlds, enchanting universes for personal bouquets.

Why not have an arrangement for the boat or for the car? Why not take a tiny vase on your next business trip and see what local plant material can be found to add a personal touch to a hotel room?

The setting will dictate what arrangement it will welcome. A dark, mysterious arrangement is not going to feel at home in a pastel setting of delicate objects. A rustic one will seem needlessly humble in a glittery, futuristic space. Use the settings as the inspiration for the arrangements. In an environment of edgy, minimalist slickness, do something punchy with the flowers: splash bold, brilliant colors in a neutral setting. Or echo subtlety with subtlety. In a setting that contains objects of differing ages and styles, joined by color and an abundance of surface texture, create an arrangement using the predominant color and lots of surface texture in leaf, petal, and container. If porcelains are in the setting, use the smallest as the container, matching flowers to the porcelain design, and use the larger porcelains for support elements, backdrop, and ambiance.

An arrangement, considered with its setting, will suggest stands and accessories that contribute to the final effect. A small picture, screen, fan, or plate can serve as an enhancing backdrop. Add only what brings life, strength, vitality to the whole. The test: the arrangement should lose something if you remove the stand or accessory.

Stands and bases turn the arrangement into a piece of sculpture. A tall stand will raise the flowers closer to eye level, a dark stand will give a feeling of weight, a clear one makes the arrangement seem to float.

Round Chinese carved-wood stands and Japanese wood scrolls can be bought in department stores and gift shops. A slab of burled wood or piece of well-sanded lumber is easily made into an attractive stand simply by staining or painting it. Stone, plastic, glass, crystal, and metal are all useful and attractive as stand materials. A piece of felt glued to the underside will keep these materials from scratching and sliding.

Accessories such as small stones, tree bark, mosses, tiny shells, and beach glass also can contribute to the arrangement. They are not added as afterthoughts. Rather, accessories work as integral components of the ensemble. Accessories serve as transitions, bridges for the eye, which tie one object to another. They help unify the objects or add dramatic impact.

Accessories are often used at the base of the container, between the container and stand, or around the container. Natural material can be used *in* the container to hide the holder not covered by flowers or leaves.

Accessories are finishing touches—the punctuation mark at the

*A faux marbre shelf above a dressing table displays primroses
and a few budding twigs in an English pottery vase.*

A mixed bunch on a dinner table for one includes "The Fairy" rose, asters, baby's breath, side shoots of celosia and sedum, all in a wicker basket.

end of a sentence. Personally, I am partial to the polished black stones from Japan that can be found in gardening and Oriental shops.

Ribbons have a history of dubious merit as accessories in formula flower arrangements, but I hesitate to dismiss them outright. Discretion, subtlety, and imagination are important in choosing any accessory—a double dose of all these is recommended when considering a ribbon to work with. Lovely copper-mesh ribbon with a subtle shimmer could be wonderful with mauve and rust chrysanthemums, for instance.

The ability to delight in small pleasures, to be charmed and even moved by what one can hold in one's hand, to experience, however fleetingly, a bit of childlike wonder, is a quality to be nurtured. And miniature arrangements—bits of tiny perfection, dazzling color, a punch to our senses—are adult expressions of that quality. Awkward as we all sometimes are, if we yield to our inner store of playfulness, with beginner's luck or practiced hand, with help from the flowers themselves, we can create and savor our own small and beautiful arrangements.

*For the automobile, an arrangement of
white heather and freesia is placed in a wood bucket.*

*A simple, classic small teacup holds tiny
carnations, wax flowers, and Peruvian lilies.*

RECOMMENDED READING LIST

Some people turn to mysteries, others cookbooks, for an enjoyable read. For me, give me a gardening book, especially one by Beverley Nichols, Gertrude Jekyll, or Vita Sackville-West. They're old and out of print now but they get reprinted from time to time, and most of them are in the public libraries. For specific information, I suggest the following books.

Foster, H. Lincoln. *Rock Gardening, A Guide to Growing Wildflowers in the American Garden.* Boston: Houghton Mifflin Company, 1968.

Martin, W. Keble. *The Concise British Flora in Color.* London: Ebury Press and Michael Joseph, 1965. An English vicar spent his long life making beautiful watercolors of native plants—over 1,400 species—reproduced here. This is not a book to carry on country walks but to turn to later as a reference.

Mitchell, Peter. *Great Flower Painters: Four Centuries of Floral Art.* Woodstock, NY: The Overlook Press, 1973. This is a collection of European floral paintings, with emphasis on seventeenth- and eighteenth-century Dutch painters.

Constance Spry School, London. *Constance Spry's Encyclopedia of Flower Arranging.* New York: Crown Publishers, Inc., 1972. The arrangements may look dated, but the information, especially on conditioning methods for different flowers, is hard to fault.

Time-Life. *Encyclopedia of Gardening.* Alexandria, VA: Time-Life Books. This is a series, started in the 1970s, numbering more than twenty volumes, with each volume devoted to a single subject, including *Miniatures and Bonsai.*

CATALOGS

Logee's Greenhouses, 55 North Street, Danielson, CT 06239. Lists of begonias, geraniums, and rare plants, including twenty varieties of fuschia and twelve jasmines. $2.50.

Geo. W. Park Seed Co., Inc., Cokesbury Road, Greenwood, SC 29647. Seeds for flowers, vegetables, herbs, and wild flowers. This illustrated catalog is free for the writing.

Thompson & Morgan, Inc., P.O. Box 100, Farmingdale, NJ 07727 (U.S. address). A catalog of trees, shrubs, greenhouse plants, vegetables, and flowers to grow from seed, available free from this famous English seed house.

The Wayside Gardens, Inc., Hodges, SC 29695. Two handsome issues a year (for a small price) filled with equally handsome plants for the gardener and arranger.

ACKNOWLEDGMENTS

I would like to thank Mr. John Esten, Mr. and Mrs. Ronald Garfunkel, Mr. and Mrs. Frederick R. Selch, Mr. and Mrs. George Shear, and Mr. and Mrs. Wm. Dwight Warren, for graciously allowing photographs to be taken in their houses or apartments; and Mr. Peter Brown of Park Ward Motors, Inc., for the "loan" of the Rolls-Royce Corniche. My thanks also to friends who provided props and cut flowers. I am especially grateful to Christine Begole for her invaluable skill in preparing the manuscript.